INSPIRED MEDITATIONS
BOOK I

WHISPERS: A JOURNALING WORKBOOK

SONJA TRISTAN

CASA
TORRES

PUBLISHING

Inspired Meditations, Book I, *Whispers*

Copyright c. 2021

Published by Casa Torres Publishing 2022

Cover Design: Timothy Tristan, Renaissance Artist, timothytristan.com

Cover Photo courtesy of: Kenneth Lee, Landscape Photographer

Description and Biography contributions: Nikki Fuzell and Marcia Stoeckel

Consultant: Racquel TW, Wild Horses Press, wildhorsespress.com

Formatting: Nate Scott, Wild Horses Press

For permission requests or inquiries, contact: Casa Torres Publishing at casatorrespublishing@gmail.com, or visit: casatorrespublishing.com

Disclaimer. The author of this book does not dispense medical advice or other professional advice or prescribe the use of any technique as a form of diagnosis or treatment for any physical, emotional, mental, spiritual or medical condition. The intent of the author is to offer information based on their experience. If you do anything suggested in this book, the publisher and the author, the distributors and bookstores, present this information for entertainment and information purposes only. This book presents the thoughts; opinions, feelings, experiences of the author and you are responsible if you choose to do anything based on what you read or the writing exercises. The publisher, author and bookseller assume no responsibility for the direct or indirect consequences of any material obtained, the reader should consult their medical, health, spiritual or other professional before adopting any of the suggestions in this book or drawing references from it, from the writing exercises or from your writings obtained from the writing exercises.

First Edition 2022

Softcover ISBN 979-8-9856271-0-7

E-Book ISBN 979-8-9856271-1-4

The author has made every effort to provide accurate contact information at the time of publication. Neither the author nor the publisher assumes any responsibility for errors or changes that occur after publication. Further, the publisher does not have any control over and does not assume any responsibility for author or third-party websites or their content.

For my Mom,
My Strength and Inspiration

For my Dad,
Such a rock and teacher!

For God
Ever Guiding and Loving

CONTENTS

INTRODUCTION

The following Inspired Meditations are adapted from practicing prayer and meditation for many years. You may notice the meditations are in the form of an answer to the question, "God, how may I be of loving service to you today?" The meditations I've selected for inclusion in this book series have helped me in numerous ways; they are always just what I need to read, hear, learn, discover, or be reminded of. The journaling workbook questions that follow the meditations, I designed, to help enrich your experience with the meditation.

Give yourself the gift of doing the daily writing exercise for each inspired meditation. Stick with it, one each day. If you're not connecting with the meditation for the day, I encourage you to ask God the same question, "how may I be of loving service to you today", pause for a moment, then write down what comes to you. Next, you'll do the writing exercise based on your inspired meditation. Some days there will be an inspired poem to write on. You'll do the same writing exercise for the poems.

The Inspired Meditations and Poems will help you to focus on faith and trust in God, and in His ever-unfolding plan. It is my hope that you enjoy each meditation and are blessed and grow as is intended by our Creator.

With love,

Sonja Tristan

HOW TO GET THE MOST OUT OF
'INSPIRED MEDITATIONS, BOOK I, WHISPERS'

One way to use this book is to read one page per day. Meditate on it for a few seconds, or minutes, then, do the suggested writing exercise. Write down what comes to you. Write stream of consciousness. Answering the four questions for each Meditation: I think, I feel, I am, and God is. No editing, no filtering and no judging. This process of meditating and writing may reveal a deeper meaning for you. You may want to have an Inspired Meditation sharing partner. Sharing what you've each written can be a beneficial experience for both of you.

Whether doing the writing exercise on your own, or with another, be courageous, be bold, and write. There are intentionally four lines available to write on for each question. If you'd like to write a little more, go above or below the lines, but not too much, being concise will help in sticking with the daily routine. Whatever time of the day you dedicate to do the reading, meditating and writing exercise, do your best to be consistent to get the most benefit. Make this your special time. Light a candle, have a cup of tea, sit outdoors in nature if that's possible and enjoyable for you. Some people like to write while commuting to or from work, as long as you're not driving. Find what time of day works best for you and dedicate yourself to this self-loving practice. Give yourself this gift, because you're worth it!

This is the first book in a three-part series. It covers January through April, at the suggested rate of one Inspired Meditation per day.

After Book I, there is Book II and Book III. It's best to go in order. You could write in the book, (if it's your own personal copy), or in a separate notebook, either way is good, just write. I suggest you start again each year with Book I, then II and III. This way you keep it fresh and see how you and your life changes from year to year. You could save your writings, but don't need to in order to be aware you're changing. You could begin any day of the year. Whatever day of the year you begin, that's your Inspired Messages New Year.

Best wishes on your journey, now let's get started.

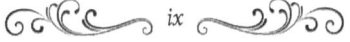 *ix*

"If we wish to make any progress in the service of God, we must begin every day of our life with new eagerness. We must keep ourselves in the presence of God as much as possible, and have no other view or end in all our actions but the divine honor."

- Saint Charles Borromeo

1. Walk, breathe, walk – will do wonders. You are loved.

I think

_____

_____

_____

_____

I feel

_____

_____

_____

_____

I am

_____

_____

_____

_____

God is

_____

_____

_____

_____

2. Mindful self-care serves me. Be in the day, the moment. I am with you.

I think

_____

_____

_____

_____

I feel

_____

_____

_____

_____

I am

_____

_____

_____

_____

God is

_____

_____

_____

_____

3. Stay warm and cozy, relax, and be in love. This is how to best serve me today.

I think

_____

_____

_____

_____

I feel

_____

_____

_____

_____

I am

_____

_____

_____

_____

God is

_____

_____

_____

_____

4. Work on creating artistically my child. Whether that's drawing, writing, painting, building mud pies, dancing, have fun. I am with you.

I think

_____

_____

_____

_____

I feel

_____

_____

_____

_____

I am

_____

_____

_____

_____

God is

_____

_____

_____

_____

5. I am here for you. Stay mindful of me throughout the day.

I think

_____

_____

_____

_____

I feel

_____

_____

_____

_____

I am

_____

_____

_____

_____

God is

_____

_____

_____

_____

6. Release, let go of, and donate unused or unneeded things. Keep what you love and need. I am with you my child.

I think

_____

_____

_____

_____

I feel

_____

_____

_____

_____

I am

_____

_____

_____

_____

God is

_____

_____

_____

_____

7. As you continue to ask me, I shall continue to help you. Forget not that I forsake thee not.

I think

_____

_____

_____

_____

I feel

_____

_____

_____

_____

I am

_____

_____

_____

_____

God is

_____

_____

_____

_____

8. Ask for help. Don't go it alone. You are not an island. I am with you my beautiful child.

I think

_____

_____

_____

_____

I feel

_____

_____

_____

_____

I am

_____

_____

_____

_____

God is

_____

_____

_____

_____

9. Rest well child. Best way to live the day is when you are well rested.

I think

_____

_____

_____

_____

I feel

_____

_____

_____

_____

I am

_____

_____

_____

_____

God is

_____

_____

_____

_____

10. All in its own time. I will provide the energy and ability you require for living in joyous communion with me. You are loved.

I think

_____

_____

_____

_____

I feel

_____

_____

_____

_____

I am

_____

_____

_____

_____

God is

_____

_____

_____

_____

11. Love softly, gently, quietly. This is how I love you, my beloved child.

I think

_____

_____

_____

_____

I feel

_____

_____

_____

_____

I am

_____

_____

_____

_____

God is

_____

_____

_____

_____

12. It's time child, to receive my gifts. That is how you may be of service to me today.

I think

_____

_____

_____

_____

I feel

_____

_____

_____

_____

I am

_____

_____

_____

_____

God is

_____

_____

_____

_____

13. Serve me by caring for yourself, and please child, do it with kindness.

I think

_____

_____

_____

_____

I feel

_____

_____

_____

_____

I am

_____

_____

_____

_____

God is

_____

_____

_____

_____

14. Your efforts to connect and be one with me are work. That is your work for today. I hope it is joyful work. This is how you serve me today. You are loved.

I think

I feel

I am

God is

---

15. Leave each to his own, don't try to fix, change anyone. Leave that to me. Stay focused on the prize, your relationship with me.

I think

_____

_____

_____

_____

I feel

_____

_____

_____

_____

I am

_____

_____

_____

_____

God is

_____

_____

_____

_____

16. Relax, spend time outdoors today. Serve me this way child – be delighted in nature. I am with you.

I think

_____

_____

_____

_____

I feel

_____

_____

_____

_____

I am

_____

_____

_____

_____

God is

_____

_____

_____

_____

17. Love is the key. It is strong. Love is my strength, for you my child.

I think

_____

_____

_____

_____

I feel

_____

_____

_____

_____

I am

_____

_____

_____

_____

God is

_____

_____

_____

_____

18. Stay in middle of the herd, where there is genuine support and understanding during this time of change. You are most loved.

I think

_____

_____

_____

_____

I feel

_____

_____

_____

_____

I am

_____

_____

_____

_____

God is

_____

_____

_____

_____

19. You are pleasant. Trust. I am with you.

I think

_____

_____

_____

_____

I feel

_____

_____

_____

_____

I am

_____

_____

_____

_____

God is

_____

_____

_____

_____

20. I am with you, I am with you, I am with you. Now, always.

I think

_____

_____

_____

_____

I feel

_____

_____

_____

_____

I am

_____

_____

_____

_____

God is

_____

_____

_____

_____

21. Stretch body and mind. Does both good, clears the cobwebs. I am with you.

I think

_____

_____

_____

_____

I feel

_____

_____

_____

_____

I am

_____

_____

_____

_____

God is

_____

_____

_____

_____

22. Willingness creates the space for me to come in. Are you willing to love and live in peace and joy? I know it's not always easy, but be willing and a path shall be made. You are loved and I am with you my sweet precious child.

I think

_____

_____

_____

_____

I feel

_____

_____

_____

_____

I am

_____

_____

_____

God is

_____

_____

_____

23. Breathe, slow down, be in quiet – in this way you can feel me as one with you. You shall live more fully. You are more beneficial to others and me when you're peaceful in mind and body. Thank you for welcoming me to live with you, in you, and through you. You are most loved.

I think

_____

_____

_____

_____

I feel

_____

_____

_____

_____

I am

_____

_____

_____

God is

_____

_____

_____

24. Drink fresh water and go for a walk when possible. It refreshes body, mind and spirit. You are loved.

I think

_____

_____

_____

_____

I feel

_____

_____

_____

_____

I am

_____

_____

_____

_____

God is

_____

_____

_____

_____

25. ROUND THE BEND

As I round the bend
I wonder
I trust
Around the bend
I am safe

I think

_____

_____

_____

_____

I feel

_____

_____

_____

_____

I am

_____

_____

_____

God is

_____

_____

_____

26. Stretch body and heart follows. You are loved.

I think

_____

_____

_____

_____

I feel

_____

_____

_____

_____

I am

_____

_____

_____

_____

God is

_____

_____

_____

_____

27. Trust. I am always on time, and I am always with you.

I think

_____

_____

_____

_____

I feel

_____

_____

_____

_____

I am

_____

_____

_____

_____

God is

_____

_____

_____

_____

28. Read what moves your heart my beloved. Read for fun, for learning, for joy.

I think

_____

_____

_____

_____

I feel

_____

_____

_____

_____

I am

_____

_____

_____

_____

God is

_____

_____

_____

_____

29. Timing is mine. Trust. I am with you.

I think

_____

_____

_____

_____

I feel

_____

_____

_____

_____

I am

_____

_____

_____

_____

God is

_____

_____

_____

_____

30. Show up with me today, every day, but let's do today, today. You are loved.

I think

_____

_____

_____

_____

I feel

_____

_____

_____

_____

I am

_____

_____

_____

_____

God is

_____

_____

_____

_____

31. I am here, I am here, I am here. Thank you for inviting me to be with you in all you do. Your presence is as much a gift to me as you say my presence is a gift to you. A present indeed my beloved!

I think

_____

_____

_____

_____

I feel

_____

_____

_____

_____

I am

_____

_____

_____

_____

God is

_____

_____

_____

_____

32. Be of service and receive services in healthy proportion. Take it easy. No rushing about dearest. Pause and breathe slowly. I am with you.

I think

_____

_____

_____

_____

I feel

_____

_____

_____

_____

I am

_____

_____

_____

_____

God is

_____

_____

_____

_____

33. Small actions are enough most of the time. Trust.

I think

_____

_____

_____

_____

I feel

_____

_____

_____

_____

I am

_____

_____

_____

_____

God is

_____

_____

_____

_____

34. Mindful consciousness this week with appointments dearest. Be where you are.

I think

_____

_____

_____

_____

I feel

_____

_____

_____

_____

I am

_____

_____

_____

_____

God is

_____

_____

_____

_____

35. Slow down and get more done, the turtle wins the race. I am with you.

I think

_____

_____

_____

_____

I feel

_____

_____

_____

_____

I am

_____

_____

_____

_____

God is

_____

_____

_____

_____

36. I only can help as much as you let go. Trust and have faith dearest.

I think

_____

_____

_____

_____

I feel

_____

_____

_____

_____

I am

_____

_____

_____

_____

God is

_____

_____

_____

_____

37. Be not content with so little, be content with all your needs met. You are loved.

I think

_____

_____

_____

_____

I feel

_____

_____

_____

_____

I am

_____

_____

_____

_____

God is

_____

_____

_____

_____

38. You're resting and trusting more. Very nice. I am with you, always.

I think

_____

_____

_____

_____

I feel

_____

_____

_____

_____

I am

_____

_____

_____

_____

God is

_____

_____

_____

_____

39. Listen and learn. There is a time for talking, and a time for listening. I am with you dearest.

I think

_____

_____

_____

_____

I feel

_____

_____

_____

_____

I am

_____

_____

_____

_____

God is

_____

_____

_____

_____

40. Futile is soloship. With others or with me is not futile. You are loved.

I think

_____

_____

_____

_____

I feel

_____

_____

_____

_____

I am

_____

_____

_____

_____

God is

_____

_____

_____

_____

41. Sing. Let's sing. Matters not what; let's just sing for a few minutes until your heart is content.

I think

_____

_____

_____

_____

I feel

_____

_____

_____

_____

I am

_____

_____

_____

_____

God is

_____

_____

_____

_____

42. Dance, sing, play. We play together. Work is work and play is play. Sometimes work is play and vice-versa, sometimes play is work. I am with you always-dearest child.

I think

_____

_____

_____

_____

I feel

_____

_____

_____

_____

I am

_____

_____

_____

_____

God is

_____

_____

_____

_____

43. Being of loving service to yourself is service. You're worth the effort dearest.

I think

_____

_____

_____

_____

I feel

_____

_____

_____

_____

I am

_____

_____

_____

_____

God is

_____

_____

_____

_____

44. Listening and waiting are Godly skills as much as speaking up and taking action.

I think

_____

_____

_____

_____

I feel

_____

_____

_____

_____

I am

_____

_____

_____

_____

God is

_____

_____

_____

_____

45. Pay bills what you can this day. Pray, and keep pencil sharpened. (That means keep skills sharp.)

I think

_____

_____

_____

_____

I feel

_____

_____

_____

_____

I am

_____

_____

_____

_____

God is

_____

_____

_____

_____

46. Touch the ground and connect with earth. Maybe touch or hug a tree. Ahh what love is in this!

I think

_____

_____

_____

_____

I feel

_____

_____

_____

_____

I am

_____

_____

_____

_____

God is

_____

_____

_____

_____

47. Forever is not your concern. Be here, now, with me. You are loved.

I think

_____

_____

_____

_____

I feel

_____

_____

_____

_____

I am

_____

_____

_____

_____

God is

_____

_____

_____

_____

48. Honor your feelings, listen to them, allow and share them with another. To make sense of them. But know dearest, feelings don't always make sense, and that's ok. I am with you my beloved child.

I think

_____

_____

_____

_____

I feel

_____

_____

_____

_____

I am

_____

_____

_____

_____

God is

_____

_____

_____

_____

49. Serve me with smiles and kindness today, when you look in the mirror, smile and say something kind to yourself.

I think

_____

_____

_____

_____

I feel

_____

_____

_____

_____

I am

_____

_____

_____

_____

God is

_____

_____

_____

_____

50. **RISE**

Don't compete with God.
God meets you where you're at,
at point of your will.
not because He is weak,
but because He is strong.
Your will creates chaos, pain, misery and destruction.
It requires God's help and guidance.
God doesn't compete with the former.
He has overcome them.
Gods' way is strength, power, love and mercy.
Rise above, with God,
And be free.

I think

_____

_____

I feel

_____

_____

I am

_____

_____

God is

_____

_____

51. Hold steadfast to your faith. Pray for help in this endeavor. You are loved.

I think

_____

_____

_____

_____

I feel

_____

_____

_____

_____

I am

_____

_____

_____

_____

God is

_____

_____

_____

_____

52. Courage, doesn't always feel good. It can feel scary. I am with you beloved.

I think

_____

_____

_____

_____

I feel

_____

_____

_____

_____

I am

_____

_____

_____

_____

God is

_____

_____

_____

_____

53. Awaken, pray, dress, work, eat, play. This is enough for today my child.

I think

_____

_____

_____

_____

I feel

_____

_____

_____

_____

I am

_____

_____

_____

_____

God is

_____

_____

_____

_____

54. Follow the winners, and judge not the non-winners today. For all are winners on a different day. Even this day the seeming loser, is yet a winner to me. You are loved.

I think

_____

_____

_____

_____

I feel

_____

_____

_____

_____

I am

_____

_____

_____

_____

God is

_____

_____

_____

_____

55. Ask for help. I am with you, always.

I think

_____

_____

_____

_____

I feel

_____

_____

_____

_____

I am

_____

_____

_____

_____

God is

_____

_____

_____

_____

56. Rest more, you know this, let slumber restore you.

I think

_____

_____

_____

_____

I feel

_____

_____

_____

_____

I am

_____

_____

_____

_____

God is

_____

_____

_____

_____

57. I am with you child, now, always. Say hello to me, that's your big task today dearest. You are loved.

I think

_____

_____

_____

_____

I feel

_____

_____

_____

_____

I am

_____

_____

_____

_____

God is

_____

_____

_____

_____

58. Tasks are service to me, by my power, not yours.

I think

_____

_____

_____

_____

I feel

_____

_____

_____

_____

I am

_____

_____

_____

_____

God is

_____

_____

_____

_____

59. Rest well; I am with you in rest too. Lots of fun to come child.

I think

_____

_____

_____

_____

I feel

_____

_____

_____

_____

I am

_____

_____

_____

_____

God is

_____

_____

_____

_____

60. Your trust is in me, for this alone I rejoice my beloved.

I think

_____

_____

_____

_____

I feel

_____

_____

_____

_____

I am

_____

_____

_____

_____

God is

_____

_____

_____

_____

61. Self-care is care to you, community, and me. We are one in community.

I think

_____

_____

_____

_____

I feel

_____

_____

_____

_____

I am

_____

_____

_____

_____

God is

_____

_____

_____

_____

62. A field that takes rest yields finer crops. Rest well, for this week I have work for you. We are a team at your invitation. I am with you.

I think

_____

_____

_____

_____

I feel

_____

_____

_____

_____

I am

_____

_____

_____

_____

God is

_____

_____

_____

_____

63. All is well, even when it isn't. You are most loved.

I think

_____

_____

_____

_____

I feel

_____

_____

_____

_____

I am

_____

_____

_____

_____

God is

_____

_____

_____

_____

64. Lighter schedule, lighter you, more room for me. You are greatly loved.

I think

_____

_____

_____

_____

I feel

_____

_____

_____

_____

I am

_____

_____

_____

_____

God is

_____

_____

_____

_____

65. Love is mindful presence that where you are, I am. Show up with me well rested, and you shall weary not this day. I am with you.

I think

_____

_____

_____

_____

I feel

_____

_____

_____

_____

I am

_____

_____

_____

_____

God is

_____

_____

_____

_____

66. Figuring it out is for me. Follow direction. You are loved.

I think

_____

_____

_____

_____

I feel

_____

_____

_____

_____

I am

_____

_____

_____

_____

God is

_____

_____

_____

_____

67. On track dearest. Stay the course. You are dearly loved.

I think

_____

_____

_____

_____

I feel

_____

_____

_____

_____

I am

_____

_____

_____

_____

God is

_____

_____

_____

_____

68. I am here, I am here with you. Difficulties are being brought out to purge and remove what is not best for you. To propel you forward out of the dark and into the light. You are not alone; you are dearly loved.

I think

_____

_____

_____

_____

I feel

_____

_____

_____

_____

I am

_____

_____

_____

God is

_____

_____

_____

69. This is the day to let go of ambitions that are not serving your inner and outer peace. Dearest child, I walk with you always.

I think

_____

_____

_____

_____

I feel

_____

_____

_____

_____

I am

_____

_____

_____

_____

God is

_____

_____

_____

_____

70. Now that you have more faith and trust in me is the reason for the peace you feel. Sing praises for this gift dearest.

I think

_____

_____

_____

_____

I feel

_____

_____

_____

_____

I am

_____

_____

_____

_____

God is

_____

_____

_____

_____

71. As you give to the world, so the world is giving to you. You are a helpful person and are attracting helpful people. This is the way of connection, caring, in giving and receiving. A loving cycle dearest.

I think

_____

_____

_____

_____

I feel

_____

_____

_____

_____

I am

_____

_____

_____

_____

God is

_____

_____

_____

_____

72. Forgive, forgive, forgive yourself and others. Now is the time. You are loved.

I think

_____

_____

_____

_____

I feel

_____

_____

_____

_____

I am

_____

_____

_____

_____

God is

_____

_____

_____

_____

73. Assume no credit for your gifts, blessings, joy, miracles - for all glory and credit is mine.

I think

_____

_____

_____

_____

I feel

_____

_____

_____

_____

I am

_____

_____

_____

_____

God is

_____

_____

_____

_____

74. I love you my child today, tomorrow, always - unchanged from the beginning of time through eternity. I am here, I am here with you.

I think

_____

_____

_____

_____

I feel

_____

_____

_____

_____

I am

_____

_____

_____

_____

God is

_____

_____

_____

_____

75. This is the dawn of another 24hrs and I encourage you to walk hand in hand with me. I thank you for showing up for you and for me – and truly, we are one anyhow.

I think

_____

_____

_____

_____

I feel

_____

_____

_____

_____

I am

_____

_____

_____

_____

God is

_____

_____

_____

_____

76. Today and each today, choose me, I choose you dearest.

I think

_____

_____

_____

_____

I feel

_____

_____

_____

_____

I am

_____

_____

_____

_____

God is

_____

_____

_____

_____

77. VOICE

Soft, loud
Breeze, wind
Real, false
Left, right
Speak
be kind
be true
be free
use your voice
shout
whisper
be silent
either way, dearest~
you are heard
always.

I think

_____

_____

I feel

_____

_____

I am

_____

_____

God is

_____

_____

78. Forgive yourself. I forgive you; you are too harsh with yourself and this doesn't serve me. Forgiveness does.

I think

_____

_____

_____

_____

I feel

_____

_____

_____

_____

I am

_____

_____

_____

_____

God is

_____

_____

_____

_____

79. There are no lies in spirit, only truth. You are near and dear child, always, in all ways.

I think

_____

_____

_____

_____

I feel

_____

_____

_____

_____

I am

_____

_____

_____

_____

God is

_____

_____

_____

_____

80. Be kind today to yourself. Starting now. If you forget, begin again. You are loved.

I think

_____

_____

_____

_____

I feel

_____

_____

_____

_____

I am

_____

_____

_____

_____

God is

_____

_____

_____

_____

81. You must not belittle me by judging yourself or another, or you judge me in so doing. You are human and all is well dearest.

I think

_____

_____

_____

_____

I feel

_____

_____

_____

_____

I am

_____

_____

_____

_____

God is

_____

_____

_____

_____

82. Willingness to commune with me is where we are at, and it is good. You are my beloved.

I think

_____

_____

_____

_____

I feel

_____

_____

_____

_____

I am

_____

_____

_____

_____

God is

_____

_____

_____

_____

83. Go forth and be in your heart equal among all, my beloved. Equally beloved dearest.

I think

_____

_____

_____

_____

I feel

_____

_____

_____

_____

I am

_____

_____

_____

_____

God is

_____

_____

_____

_____

84. You have been jealous in the past, maybe even now. Acceptance is your new code, of yourself. All is well.

I think

_____

_____

_____

_____

I feel

_____

_____

_____

_____

I am

_____

_____

_____

_____

God is

_____

_____

_____

_____

85. I know you and all you need. Trust in me. You are loved.

I think

_____

_____

_____

_____

I feel

_____

_____

_____

_____

I am

_____

_____

_____

_____

God is

_____

_____

_____

_____

86. Where you have been lazy is assessed in error. Your claims to laziness are in fact, balance. I am with you and I guide you – so judge me not, judge you not, trust.

I think

_____

_____

_____

_____

I feel

_____

_____

_____

_____

I am

_____

_____

_____

_____

God is

_____

_____

_____

_____

87. You are doing a good job. The work is not in vain, nor is it vanity. You are here for me and to serve me and I acknowledge you and your efforts. I know your concern, worry, fear, and ask that you give them to me. Let me have their weight and burden and I shall be glad to solve and resolve all of it. Happiness, freedom and joy are the state I desire to see you my child experience each new sun up to slumber. To slumber in joy and peace is the way with me. I am with you.

I think

_____

_____

_____

I feel

_____

_____

_____

I am

_____

_____

_____

God is

_____

_____

_____

88. Suddenly to some, slower with others. All is well, even when it isn't.

I think

_____

_____

_____

_____

I feel

_____

_____

_____

_____

I am

_____

_____

_____

_____

God is

_____

_____

_____

_____

89. How can I convince you that I am here, with you, in every now? There is an answer. Stop, and listen. Listen not with your physical ears – listen with your breath. Listen to the flow of your blood moving through your body, listen with your skin – feel me – this is how to hear me – by feeling me. Listen with your heart, and know dearest, I am here.

I think

_____

_____

_____

_____

I feel

_____

_____

_____

_____

I am

_____

_____

_____

God is

_____

_____

_____

90. Dearest I am here for you and your fellows on this path and I am glad for all your efforts to know me, follow me and to serve me.

I think

_____

_____

_____

_____

I feel

_____

_____

_____

_____

I am

_____

_____

_____

_____

God is

_____

_____

_____

_____

91. Your light shines brighter, know your light is and shall always be as bright as the day you began in the world – it has never dimmed – nor will it ever. Difference is it shines to you and your fellows even brighter as peace is restored. You are my beloved.

I think

_____

_____

_____

_____

I feel

_____

_____

_____

_____

I am

_____

_____

_____

_____

God is

_____

_____

_____

92. Meditate on what level of love is necessary to heal and transform. Then take out the trash. Get on with your day my dearest child.

I think

_____

_____

_____

_____

I feel

_____

_____

_____

_____

I am

_____

_____

_____

_____

God is

_____

_____

_____

_____

93. Be gentle but disciplined with yourself, very gentle and loving, kind as well, always. Meditate on how this will look, feel, sound. Hint, it will look, feel, and sound very beautiful.

I think

_____

_____

_____

_____

I feel

_____

_____

_____

_____

I am

_____

_____

_____

_____

God is

_____

_____

_____

_____

94. Everyone and Everything – Bless everyone and everything in prayer and thought. Then leave them to me.

I think

_____

_____

_____

_____

I feel

_____

_____

_____

_____

I am

_____

_____

_____

_____

God is

_____

_____

_____

_____

95. I am here with you now. This I would have you do, draw nearer to me with all you heart. You are loved.

I think

_____

_____

_____

_____

I feel

_____

_____

_____

_____

I am

_____

_____

_____

_____

God is

_____

_____

_____

_____

96. Trust in me and the things I accomplish. You are loved.

I think

_____

_____

_____

_____

I feel

_____

_____

_____

_____

I am

_____

_____

_____

_____

God is

_____

_____

_____

_____

97. Confidence is occasionally earned, yet usually gifted by me with desire of one's innermost yearnings. I provide. Ask and I shall provide you with confidence, as you desire. You have been gifted with confidence for many years, because you desired it with sincerity and with the intention to serve. You underestimate your confidence and in so doing deny the gift I have bestowed in great measure. Not in all areas at once, where would the balance be in that? Indeed, I will grant you more, as you desire in new arenas. Prepare to receive dearest child, you are my beloved.

I think

_____

_____

_____

I feel

_____

_____

_____

I am

_____

_____

_____

God is

_____

_____

_____

98. Success and prosperity are yours now. They are mine and they are yours. Look around, see it, see me, accept this deep in your awareness and you will join me in this truth. You are loved.

I think

_____

_____

_____

_____

I feel

_____

_____

_____

_____

I am

_____

_____

_____

_____

God is

_____

_____

_____

_____

99. Desire only to serve me. To be close to me. I am here for you beloved.

I think

_____

_____

_____

_____

I feel

_____

_____

_____

_____

I am

_____

_____

_____

_____

God is

_____

_____

_____

_____

100. Yes beloved, here we are as one on this day. I have created the heavens, stars and earth for you. You are my beloved. I have loved you before time and I shall l love you for eternity.

I think

_____

_____

_____

_____

I feel

_____

_____

_____

_____

I am

_____

_____

_____

_____

God is

_____

_____

_____

_____

101. BE STILL AND KNOW THAT I AM GOD

Be still and know that I am
Be still and know
Be still
Be

I think

_____

_____

_____

I feel

_____

_____

_____

I am

_____

_____

_____

God is

_____

_____

_____

102. You ask for direction child. I appreciate your desire for my guidance. Pause, pray, dress, eat, breathe, go about your daily tasks and keep your eyes, ears, mind and heart open. You are loved.

I think

_____

_____

_____

_____

I feel

_____

_____

_____

_____

I am

_____

_____

_____

_____

God is

_____

_____

_____

_____

103. I rejoice in a grateful receiver of my gifts such as you are. There are gifts in the seemingly ugly. You needn't search for them, rather be grateful for everything and the gift will be revealed. You are loved dearest, always.

I think

_____

_____

_____

_____

I feel

_____

_____

_____

_____

I am

_____

_____

_____

_____

God is

_____

_____

_____

104. Release, let go, and give me all your hurts, cares, worries and fears. You are loved and never alone. I am with you, always.

I think

_____

_____

_____

_____

I feel

_____

_____

_____

_____

I am

_____

_____

_____

_____

God is

_____

_____

_____

_____

105. Taking care of yourself serves me. I will help you in this endeavor, just ask. Your physical body is a temple for me to do good in the world. Do you see child? I am with you.

I think

_____

_____

_____

_____

I feel

_____

_____

_____

_____

I am

_____

_____

_____

_____

God is

_____

_____

_____

_____

106. Be bountiful as a new natural state. Imagine it. Take time to imagine it dearest. You are loved.

I think

_____

_____

_____

_____

I feel

_____

_____

_____

_____

I am

_____

_____

_____

_____

God is

_____

_____

_____

_____

107. You are a present. For I have pre-sent you to guide the way of love for those who are to be after you. Be what you are, love, you are love and dearly loved my beloved. Love is strength, my strength. Dwell in love, in me, with me.

I think

_____

_____

_____

_____

I feel

_____

_____

_____

_____

I am

_____

_____

_____

_____

God is

_____

_____

_____

108. Being in feelings feels like me. Fear them not. Allow and holdeth back not the feeling. All things pass. All feelings pass, good or bad, allow and be at peace with me, whatever the feeling. I am with you.

I think

_____

_____

_____

_____

I feel

_____

_____

_____

_____

I am

_____

_____

_____

_____

God is

_____

_____

_____

_____

109. Be present and prosperous in all that is good, loving and kind. Be strong also, by my strength. I am with you.

I think

_____

_____

_____

_____

I feel

_____

_____

_____

_____

I am

_____

_____

_____

_____

God is

_____

_____

_____

_____

110. WHISPER
Help me, help me
I'm on my knees

Here I come
Here I go
Here, there, no where
Where did you go?
Where did I go?
Here we come
Here we go
Here, there, no where

I ran
You found me
Was I lost? I don't know
Where was I?

Look out
It's about to get better
Right here, right now

It's a thunderstorm
It's a sleepy summer day
All rolled into one

I feel a wave
It's loud, It's a whisper

I'm standing now
With You

I think

_____

_____

_____

_____

I feel

_____

_____

_____

_____

I am

_____

_____

_____

_____

God is

_____

_____

_____

_____

111. This is it sweet child, time for you to receive me and my strength, love and joy. It is not earned or a reward, rather a blessing bestowed dearest.

I think

_____

_____

_____

_____

I feel

_____

_____

_____

_____

I am

_____

_____

_____

_____

God is

_____

_____

_____

_____

112. Quiet now, sshhh – it is our time - yours and mine. Let's hang out together, be as one. We are one. I am with you, and all, simultaneously. You are all dearly loved.

I think

_____

_____

_____

_____

I feel

_____

_____

_____

_____

I am

_____

_____

_____

_____

God is

_____

_____

_____

_____

113. It is now that I am here with you beloved. Now, here. Life can be light; I can be light, as you can now see, this part of me you did not know before. Easy, breezy, cheesy, silly. I can play and have fun. Yes, there is a time for work, and definitely a time for play and laughter. Child, you are dearly loved.

I think

_____

_____

_____

_____

I feel

_____

_____

_____

_____

I am

_____

_____

_____

God is

_____

_____

_____

114. It is my design for you to work, yes, to serve, yes, and dearest, to laugh and enjoy. This is my design, you are love, you are loved, as am I. I am with you.

I think

_____

_____

_____

_____

I feel

_____

_____

_____

_____

I am

_____

_____

_____

_____

God is

_____

_____

_____

_____

115. You desire riches and wealth for peace – however, this is backwards for true and solid riches and wealth. For true wealth and riches are born of peace within.

I think

_____

_____

_____

_____

I feel

_____

_____

_____

_____

I am

_____

_____

_____

_____

God is

_____

_____

_____

_____

116. Child feel free to anger and vent to me, and then let it go. Be free through expression by writing it out to me, or speaking to me. It's good and healthy. Freedom ensured as result, safe and sound with me, soundness of mind is natural state through truth feelings expressed. You are most loved.

I think

_____

_____

_____

_____

I feel

_____

_____

_____

_____

I am

_____

_____

_____

God is

_____

_____

_____

117. You walk, I walk, you sleep – I don't. I watch over you and all, always.

I think

_____

_____

_____

_____

I feel

_____

_____

_____

_____

I am

_____

_____

_____

_____

God is

_____

_____

_____

_____

118. Trust your heart and let go, trust. All is well sweet child. Even when it isn't, it is, for I am with you. Always.

I think

_____

_____

_____

_____

I feel

_____

_____

_____

_____

I am

_____

_____

_____

_____

God is

_____

_____

_____

_____

119. Stay the course of prayer, trust, faithful actions; it gets easier my beloved. Take only this day into account, yet today is eternal. I love you dearly; you are my beloved, my heart, and my breath.

I think

_____

_____

_____

_____

I feel

_____

_____

_____

_____

I am

_____

_____

_____

_____

God is

_____

_____

_____

_____

120. This is the day I have made for you, your brothers, and your
sisters
My dearest beloved child
all are your brothers and sisters
You are all one
One heart
My heart
It is so
(child)

I think

_____

_____

_____

I feel

_____

_____

_____

I am

_____

_____

_____

God is

_____

_____

_____

"Walk cheerfully and with a sincere and open heart as much as you can, and when you cannot always maintain this holy joy, at least do not lose heart or your trust in God."

-Padre Pio

BIBLIOGRAPHY

How to Listen to God, written in the late 1930's by John E. Batterson (A personal friend of Dr. Bob's – co-founder of A.A.), *How to Listen to God*. Distributed by: Wally P., Archivist/Historian/Author, Tucson, AZ

"I studied and practiced, *How to Listen to God*, by John E. Batterson, for a few years. It helped me learn discernment and discipline. The results gave me much peace and joy.

This led me to asking the single question; God, how can I be of loving service to you today? This book series developed from my personal experience in asking this single question.

I do not claim to be endorsed by the authors or distributors of *How to Listen to God*."

- Sonja Tristan

AFTERWORD

Now that you've completed Book I, take a moment to congratulate and reward yourself, I congratulate you, and am proud of you. Reward yourself for your efforts, maybe do something fun. I'm here to encourage and cheer you on in continuing with 'Inspired Meditations, Book II, *Renaissance'*, the second book in this series, without interruption. Let's keep up the good work.

Whether you're sharing your writings with another, or keeping it to yourself, I'm glad you're showing up for yourself, one Inspired Meditation at a time, and doing the writing exercises. For as you get in touch with yourself and your relationship with God, it can be self-esteeming and revealing of deeper truths for you, having a positive effect in your life, those around you, and the world.

Peace and Blessings,

Sonja

LEGACY

This page is a special dedication for my children, grandchildren, great-grandchildren and all my descendants.

I've put these books together for you. Something of me to share with you. The meditations in this three book series have helped me form a personal relationship with God and they are a valued treasure I gift you with.

It's my hope they give you encouragement, strength, and perseverance to fulfill your dreams and goals in life. To do good, be brave, and most of all, to strengthen your faith and trust in God.

I come from a long lineage of love, strength, courage, and faith. So that means you did too! At times things were difficult and I felt alone. But I wasn't, God was always there, it just took me many years to really feel it, to know it. Looking back I see He was always there, and I'd like you to know this too, in your own way. Let these inspired meditations into your heart and know my that I am whispering my love to you, holding your hand on your journey, and giving you a gentle hug and kiss.

I loved you before you were here and you are precious.

S

ABOUT THE AUTHOR

Sonja Tristan lives in Southern California, where she enjoys spending time in nature, visiting museums and urban exploring. Her journey with religion and in seeking an understanding of the depth of God's love is another one of her greatest joys and a driving force within her. Discovering God in people, the natural environment, and in art, has proven to her, that the more one looks for God, He is to be found everywhere.

Sonja holds degrees in Liberal Arts, Humanities, Economics, and Urban Planning. This diverse background shows the passion that burns bright within her, as she seeks new and deep spiritual knowledge for personal development. This inspires her professional life and has made her a beacon of hope for many.

Success through meditation definitely quantifies Sonja's life journey of deep spiritual peace that has elevated her soul with a quiet, humble, caring truth.

When asked what prompted this book, she has said that discovering the depth of God's love has been her greatest joy and passing on His blessings to all is her greatest wish.

CONNECT: SONJA TRISTAN

https://www.sonjatristan.com

INSTAGRAM: @SonjasLALife

FACEBOOK: https://www.facebook.com/sonjatorrestristan

FOR INQUIRIES: https://CasaTorresPublishing.com

EMAIL: CasaTorresPublishing@gmail.com

www.ingramcontent.com/pod-product-compliance
Lightning Source LLC
Chambersburg PA
CBHW030310130626
46549CB00002B/796